THE LANGUAGE OF ELDORADO

For Jonathan Hill
With best wishes
— Mark McWatt
1995-01-07

Acknowledgements

Some of the poems in this collection have appeared first in the following publications: *Pathways*, *The Graham House Review*, *Kyk-Over-Al* and *Kunapipi*.

I am grateful to the Guyanese artist Stanley Greaves for his permission to use his painting 'Landscape of the Hearts and Diamonds' for the cover. Stanley Greaves has stated that this painting was inspired by Wilson Harris's novel *Heartland*.

© Mark McWatt 1994

First published in 1994 by Dangaroo Press
Australia: G.P.O. Box 1209, Sydney, New South Wales, 2001
Denmark: Pinds Hus, Geding Søvej 21, 8381 Mundelstrup
UK: P.O. Box 20, Hebden Bridge, West Yorkshire, HX7 5UZ

ISBN 1-871049-08-3
Printed in Great Britain by Villiers Publications, London N3.

THE LANGUAGE OF ELDORADO: POEMS

By Mark McWatt

Dangaroo Press

For Amparo

And For My Mother

Contents

Preface

At the centre of this collection is the longish title-poem which seeks to explore aspects of the relationship between language, landscape and the history of human settlement in Guyana. It is dedicated to Wilson Harris who has explored these ideas in much greater depth than I can and who has influenced my own thinking along these lines. This title-poem, along with the opening and closing movements of the volume (*Rivers of Dream* and *A Potaro Quartet*) carry on a concern with themes of the interior of Guyana and of the psyche that I first attempted to explore in *Interiors*. As in that collection, however, there is also another type of poem included here; the more accessible poems dealing with childhood riddles and experiences (*Under the Children*) and with the drama of everyday domestic situations and impersonations (*Masks with Voices*) are inserted between – and offer (comic?) relief from – the above-mentioned movements of poems that brood on interior landscapes. The dedications (of movements and of individual poems) are to writers whose work I admire and have learned from, and to companions in the past who shared with me some of the 'adventures' in the interior that underlie the poems themselves.

PROLOG

Then

Then were only
  the foetal islands, blue hints of
continents, protoplasmic sea,
  and winds strewn with thorns
– abrasive as radical ideologies –
  roaring in from the north,
yet containing the torn whisper,
  seeping from an older world,
of flesh too fragile for history.

Then the gathering of light
  down the cordillieras of the unknown
world, its concentration in proto-cities,
  its refraction in vast prismatic shields,
its containment in dim forests. Then
  the red urgency of blood, creating
the sacrificial time, the fascinated order
  and languages only the sun can read.

Then the osmotic assault
  of the history-mongering tribes
of Europe, with their penchant
  for names and other subtleties,
fretting about 'Indies' amidst the
  righteous bleeding, as the ruddied
occidental light, shipped home in galleons,
  leapt from divine gold and silver.
Then dead God and living kings shone
  like body and blood of stars.

Then dark dregs from yet another
  continental weariness overspread
islands and coasts, establishing hierarchies
  of sweat and bitter memory

in the name of snow-white cotton
   and sweetest sugar-cane,

Then the cruellest freedoms
   breed the cruellest nothing
as all the human crops fail in islands
   and continents; and the fearsome thorns
in the wind hook and unravel civilizations
   leaving the single endless thread
of blood-red light from which
   the sun is still suspended.

And then...

RIVERS OF DREAM

(in memory of Bernard J. Darke, S.J.)

Rivers of Dream

Rivers of dream run
in the hollow
in the hallowed
shallows
of my mind
where I often find
(and always mistake for some other)
my own phosphorescent skeleton
blundering among river rocks
and longing for the sea.

I may be you and you,
but I am never me
when the rivers of dream
run in the hollow
in the hallowed
shallows...

Amakura

Spokes of dusty light
descended from a hub above the trees
and pierced the black skin
of the river. Twin engines
of wheel and water
created an interior space
where memory now blooms
like the smell of time
in long-shut rooms.

Blue butterflies stitched the rare sunlight
to the jealous gloom of the overhanging trees
that shaped your womb of silence:
thus visual simplicities
constitute the reality
of rivers one must live by...
the way all of life, sometimes,
is reflected in an orchid – or an eye.

Men, like vivid butterflies, must
end by losing themselves
in the density of thought that surrounds you,
like those men in the beginning
(of my time, not yours) whose crude oaths
broke your silence, not your spirit,
as they searched in vain
your dark veins
for signs of Eldorado.

Yet it can not be true
to speak of silence and of you
in that same breath that stalks
the surface of your dream, like a spider...
I have only to think
of Amakura, and your distant vowels

enter my soul (inter
my soul) – a cold seepage
from an old, old world – and help shape
my life-sentence: ever
to be apart
from your sacred sibilance
and the language of my heart.

The Native of Questions

Mist on the morning river
summons a spirit of questioning
like the dawn of revolution,
as your paddle cuts water and space
like a knife of cold laughter
opening a vein of memory.

What place is this
whose shape the mist erases?
Can it ever be sculpted again
into the clarity of home?

What drums – no, what wings
are beating? And how can bird fly
to a perch no eye can see? – unless
the world's weave is being unravelled
just for me.

What fire insinuates
its damp smoke into the mist?
Or is it all smoke?
Is the world's flesh burning?

O God! O Heracleitus!
What can bone wrapped in smoke aspire to?
And who asks these questions?
– Is it I? Or you?

Later, when you look
for the native of questions
you find he has already become the answer
to a riddle that is irrelevant...
as the bright dog of sunlight
tears the morning mist
at the fiery brink of the waterfall:
your final comic twist.

Ibis

A flock of ibis, a fleece of morning cloud –
white host for the blood-red wings,
a foretaste of the rising sun, like wine,
amidst the mangroves' green and gold
and the river's tidal swelling...

Ibis wings set on scarlet fire
in a world as yet untouched by sun,
and their phoenix-dance on the polished river
suggest twin themes of an old desire:
the blood of God and the heart of man.

White and red, the cloud on fire:
ibis over the green-gold land,
teaching the arrow and the eye
the habit of reaching ever higher.
All pilgrim paths and songs of love
lead to ibis and cloud above:
the sphere to which all minds aspire.

The Girl at Santa Rosa

The girl at Santa Rosa
moved like a snake,
the moon on her shoulder
as she paddled, stirred the gloom
of the Moruka.

We were coming too soon.

The girl at Santa Rosa
danced like a snake,
crawling under my skin like the music:
warm flesh and cold flakes of moonlight
conspired to take us in.

We were going too soon.

The girl at Santa Rosa
held my hand
all the way back up the river
which twisted and turned like a snake
under the moon.

We had drowned each snake-like other
in the moonlit tide of a moment
that came and went too soon.

When I Loved You: Four Memories

(for Linda)

I

When I loved you
time was with me always
and I let myself fall
– that easy, lilting fall into fancy –
until I knew nothing at all
but the sound of your laughter
and that voice that would call
across the misty river;
then the warm breath, the haste
of my little heart that beat
my dreams into a furious pace
before my distance from our world
shone like a tear-track down your face,
when you loved me
and time was as ebbing as the sea...

II

When I loved you
along with your old wine
you offered me
an atlas of the universe
in the shape of your body
and in return I assured you,
by subtleties of touch,
that countless other worlds exist
beneath the tarnished surfaces
of flesh and nature.

Lost in the space of love
we could have wandered forever...

but you touched a frenulum of doubt
and the universe stiffened into flesh,
its transubstantial echoes
fading on my tongue
like the taste of wine...

III

When I loved you
we ran with the dark river at night
into worlds woven just for us:
oxbows, itabos and lagoons
where love was hard and sharp-edged
with the excitement
of many imagined dangers...
until, with the help of
a sudden treason of thought
and a sliver of moon,
I caught a glimpse of your desire
in the rinse of shadows,
among flecks of foam like accusing eyes.

This was the danger least expected:
love lived on the dark river
then, in a dark moment of mind,
love died...

IV

When I loved you
was it foolish
to want more of you
than flesh or time could give?
When you took yourself away from me
for longer than I could bear,
like a foolish child I played God

and made another you
out of words and paper...

How was I to know
that this sickness would consume me
until I loved my version of you
better than your real self?
Thirty years later,
in the knowledge that you are safe
from me forever,
I'm still making and remaking you
and loving you on paper.

The Straits of Heaven

Perdus, sans mâts, sans mâts, ni fertiles îlots...
Mais, ô mon coeur, entends le chant des matelots!

– Mallarmé

Lost in the straits of heaven
with every rib cracked
and washing its red
into the sun-glazed sea:
who can patch
the punctured lung of the sky
that slowly collapses?
God's needle flashes like ship's rails
in the sunset of my eye.

She who shares the cabin of my ribs
bleeds and dies with me,
pierced by the sun's broken glass;
'The mast! The mast!' she cried.
The fallen mast trailed its drops of silver,
and she was my twin sister then,
sharing my birth, astride
my lonqest wave –
she who should have been my bride.

Seaweed, like the muse's hair,
painted a flag on her finger
thrust out of my side.
'Without the mast, O God,
who can tame your tide?'
Waves of ocean swept us and we drifted wide
of Heaven's gate – far
from every fertile island;
until baskets of stars swam
into the mortal midway of my dream.

The weight of starlight, or a devil's hand
struck and twisted our mouth
into a hollow hope and cry:
'Land!' the sailors sang for joy,
'Land!' A lizard's tail or the stump of a finger,
on which veins grew into lines of forest
and branched roots, like hair,
sucked the flesh of a continent.

'Waini! Is Waini point!'
A star stood over Waini point
as I led her up its funnel of love,
across long alluvial groins
in the damp dream of my heart;
up shell beaches, through mangrove fingers
flagged with seaweed,
into the forest of the star.
And there, on the point itself,
the rarest of blooms breathed like a child.

The flower of the universe.
It waved its petals, larger than clouds,
and poured its heavenly liquor on us;
it was my own blood which she caught
in her cupped hands.

God's needle had pierced my dreaming eye,
stitching the sailors' song and cry
into my cruellest awakening.
Listen to the sailors lost on the ocean:
'No mast to cling to, no fertile island.'

My lover heaved my cracked ribs
with her last breath and reply;
my side opened, like love's flower
and the sailors flung their plummet
through my heart
in quest of Heaven.

A Poem at Baramanni

In the resthouse at Baramanni
I kept the Tilley lamp
hissing half the night,
trying to write
my poem.
But the light
only gave a million insects
excuse for a rowdy fete;
and during their loud,
instrumental hum
not a line,
not a word would come.

When I tucked myself,
deaf/eated,
into the mosquito net,
its white enclosure mocked me
like the white, empty pages on the desk.

The river next morning
was that inspired page
I had sought to write:
A stark rendering of trees and sky,
the startling image of a bird
leaving a light, alliterative ripple
in shallows near the tall grass;
the nice parallelism of a dragon-fly
mating its own image on the river's glass.

That page, unblotted by morning mist,
was perfectly legible in the young sunshine;
and when the soft splash of a mangrove seed
initialled its near margin
with a flourish, I was no longer blind
to the happy truth

that none of the world's poems
(or that all of them)
are mine.

Heartland

(for Brian Stevenson)

We thought we had found it once
in a pool of resonant emerald
beneath an unnamed waterfall.

But who knows where, among the miles
of rotting and spawning green
is the smallest
of the concentric circles,
heart of growth or oblivion,
greenheart or granite
– and how secure
from the bleak eye of God
blue beyond the leaves?

The shifting premises of hope
wound the heart's certitudes,
as heartland swims eternally beyond place,
drowns in seas over the horizon,
hides down the path not taken when
a parrot snake shuffled across its leaves.

The heart's conception
and the heart's deception
may occur in the self-same place,
where movements in the undergrowth
are more than a fugitive breeze
but less than the breath of God.

Although it often seems we live
so that reason can erase
the numinous glyphs of love
inscribed in every landscape,
There is something *there*,
after all,

that *is* the central spider
in our web of dreams,
that weaves the net of Eldorado,
that launches the drunken boat...

There is something,
other than the setting sun,
that catches the river afire.

The Palms in Le Repentir

The magnificent palms
in Le Repentir
strut beside the narrow bridge of life,
channelling a city
through the quiet corner of its dead.
Their shadows lengthen over tombs
in the evening.
At night they become the spirits
of those buried there;
our long dead fathers, standing in line
as men here have always stood,
waiting. And the women,
they too are dredged nightly
from the river beds of memory
to flaunt their style
in the impenetrable shade of the palms:
fragile in lace, or massive
in the sackcloth of my conscience –
mothers, all of them,
their endless commandments
now leaking through the fissures of their flesh
into the swamp.

In the morning all is peace
as the palms rock their heads
of sungilt leaves and mock
the fears of life and death
that wring me to repentance:
they have no such cares
as they rejoice in ecstasies of breeze
and morning dew at their planted feet,
and are drunk, drunk deep of the seas
of purest sky-blue
– those great sentinel trees
of my memory.

Benediction

...vitam sine termino
nobis donet in patria.

The mangroves at the water's edge,
their plumbing exposed by the tide,
deride my love for this drowned place
of waist-deep mud and river so wide
the very sun is often late
for its daily death on the other side.

Yet roots and branches form the web
woven by that spider sun
to sift the alluvial souls of rivers
and trap their sins as they run
to the sea's salt, purgatorial troughs
where soul and substance become one.

And I am left on this near shore
where all the dreams of heaven start:
Who sifts the clotted sins of earth
where land and sun and river part
in obscene mangrove fingers, will find
the trifling treasure of my heart.

– I come from this, in this I move.
Blessed be this place I love.

UNDER THE CHILDREN

(for John Agard)

Under the Children

It was an afternoon of leaves when I fell
under the feet of children.
I dreamed among their legs
on which were still the stains of birth
clear as water;
I dreamt in a sunken world, subterranean city,
where the winds were shod
with the treble cries of children,
falling in my ear:
and I did not cry out then
for I had come to fulfil a long desire.

I saw each ankle-thrust
with the eyes of a snake,
their machinery of limbs kept my fires awake.
The children whistled as they trampled me to dust,
dancing. I saw the shape of love
in every pummelling fist,
in every curved instep aimed at my neck...
until the last ink-stained limb
left me dying.

There was another level, I dreamt,
deeper still, where golden sparks
came from secret furnaces
beyond the cracked walls of my first room,
blown with leaves
under the feet of children .

I heard my own voice then, light
like the flutter of fingers turning pages,
calling home:

'My mother, the children have killed me,
They have eaten me alive, mother

they have kneaded my hair into the earth
they have mocked my prophesies and my love
they have torn and bloodied my garments
they have tossed me into an inky sewer
and you were not there to rescue me,
my mother.

I boasted that you would banish them
you would bury them beneath mountains
you would drown them in the sea
you would make them fall and worship me
and feel my boot like snakes among dead leaves,
mother.'

But she was long deaf
and smiled at the children,
her own children home from school,
with wine flowing from their flesh
with the ink of life on their fingers
and the story of love on their faces.
My own mother smiled,
and the children fell into rooms,
fell onto beds,
fell on me, weary with their innocence:
and I held them all in my subterranean arms,
circled them with my veins of gold
and they were unharmed in the fiery furnace –
then I crawled out of them, like a snake.

I shone with a new skin of great beauty,
covered with patterns of ink and leaves
and footprints of gold,
to show that I was once
under the children.

Child's Play

Across the furnace of the sea
there is a land
where we could change our name
with every season.

As brother I would take your hand
in the bright bloom of spring;

and it would be the same
with summer's long days:
as a lover
you could drink my wine.

As my wetnurse in the coldest nights
you could break my body
with any stroke of genius.

There is even a season
when you would own my mind,
locked in its shell of bone
apart from reason;

and you the bride yet
of all mankind.

Such are the unnatural flowers
of a mental rhyme;
but is reality a different land,
a different time?

Philip

A young son
is an out-of-date mirror
haunting you
with images long passed:
that smooth skin that smells
like spit on glass
is another mirror's skin;
and you're caught
between twin
terrors – his future
and your past.

You know that skin will change:
burn, harden, slacken
– in a refining process –
some call it sin
but I forbear to pass
that kind of judgment,
at least while
that suspicious smile
continues to take me in.

Fairy Tale Blues

Sometimes I hear them whispering in bed
and know they're plotting to be rid of me
They gave me all these books and filled my head
with stories of lost children for a purpose
– children know all about purpose, and we dread
that fairy-tale voice that murders all our hope
and that Judas kiss that fastens us in bed.

'Don't forget to pray for Mum and Dad' they say
but I beg God to save *me* instead, from hell
and heaven: I don't want to go either way;
but God is on their side, I can tell:
I'm threatened with 'You haven't been good today'
and 'Shame! You know your mother isn't well.'
I'm small and evil and must be sent away...

So children's poems are for saying goodbye
That's why I'm writing this for all my friends;
When I'm gone you'll see, they'll mourn and sigh
and give away my things, and seek to make amends,
and their new baby will take the place of I.

Street Arab

How is the little lover taught
the secrets of an unknown art?
Mummy sends him to the shop
to buy the fish and penny-bread
and, returning idle through the desert,
He stumbles into a lost corral,
and must now tell
of Arab nights after:
in the pastures
where the horses of the moon
feed and gallop away, away...
far (for a hungry child like him)
far, far too soon.
The sailing crescent half reveals
its fields of tangled limbs
and each street-arab comes to know
(secretly) that horses are his kings.

Gull

My son brought home a seagull
with a damaged wing
his mother and sister helped
him fuss over it and feed the wild,
ungrateful thing.

They treated the raw, unfeathered
patch and tied the drooping limb
to its body with a strip of cloth;
deciding not to name him yet,
they placed him for the night
in a shoebox lined with an old towel
complete with plastic tot of water
and two smelly sprats, procured
with difficulty at such short warning.
The boy guessed all would be right,
come morning.

In fact the thing died.
when I checked before breakfast, it
was stiff, and its rank death
had already attracted a phalanx
of tiny ants. My son said nothing;
looked at it a while, then
dealt it an almighty kick, box and all
and sent it crashing into the opposite wall.

So much for the nameless bird.
Sister and mother were aghast,
upset he could be so uncaring,
But I understood why he kicked it,
and approved, beneath the mandatory frown.
I think it's right to kick at death,
especially when you're young.
He was not uncaring, what he cared for

was life, the chance to see the creature mend,
to release it and watch it soar;
the lifeless form was cruel recompense
for all the love and care he'd felt before
– and so he wanted no business
with dead things, his savage kick
focussed his argument more sharply
than these words, and I hope for him
a life as fiercely free as he had wanted
for that awkward, damaged bird.

Curlicues

From the fringe of a clearing
I watched a solitary girl
like a flowering shrub among the stern trees.

Idle, yet in her eyes a kind of caring,
waving a smouldering stick
that made curlicues in the dusk.

The flaming, fading figure eight
made with an easy sweep of her wrist
lived and died like my many loves.

My love is like a lily among thorns,
and this elfin child, playing with fire,
piercing my masks of dread.

But children tire as readily of pleasure
as of pain: a passing cloud of thought
and the stick abruptly stubbed out in the sand.

A crucifix of branches, caught on a river rock
is soon thundered over the waterfall:
so time destroys belief and the beautiful...

And we must live on, swept
endlessly over the lip of tomorrow,
and still sing of love

as our flaming images are stifled in a dust.

Observing Children

He said we must walk
to the hillside where children play
to take his mind away
from thoughts of death;
but death has many proxies,
I learnt that day.

When he stopped and looked
into the wind that carried
a coarse whisper of immortality
upon the breaths of boys,
I tugged in vain
against his train of thought
and tried to hurry him on;
But he resisted, and I understood:

It seemed a vision sent for the dying,
the viaticum of desire
before the burial of appetite.
Beyond the banalaties of love
the forgotten boyhood rite
seemed strangely violent
in his calm afternoon; it was as if
he saw convulsions of earth and sky
and the whiplash of a long lost horizon
returning to mortify
the barren hillside and the observing eye.

Figures in the field: boys –
not much younger than I – painted
in the intimate hues of his own memory
or dreams of adolescence.
He heard boyish songs of experience
shouldering between
the lips of approaching night

the frail bravado of flesh
too fragile for ecstasy,
which is at best a trick of memory.

Memory was the end of all his quests.
dry memories, and hard
like the hand that held my wrist,
apprehension tightening bone on bone,
sustaining the illusion of bodily power –
until the boys slipped
off the edge of his mind, as the yolk
of the sun slips beneath the hill
leaving the albuminous dusk
like thickening smoke in the eyes of old men,
prompting them to pain...

Back home his eyes, brightened by tears,
seemed so much purer than my own thought
that I felt the sharpest twist of shame
for having pitied an old, old child
who could see much further than I –
who had been blind for eighteen years.

THE LANGUAGE OF ELDORADO

(for Wilson Harris)

The Language of Eldorado

...Pays fameux dans les chansons,
Eldorado banal de tous les vieux garçons...

       – Baudelaire

1

Such sad faces, they tell me,
are shadows of the golden age:
Chains of events masquerading as being,
Turning the teeth of saws,
old, uttered by ageless men, spitting
into the river where the dust of forests
rides their hope's highest tide.

It was a Madonna of the adventurers
– or so I fantasized –
that lump of unknown forest wood:
the suggestion of a veiled head
and rudimentary, averted eyes.
Its shoulder, covered with notches,
told the oldest tale of Eldorado.

Loved and left by a queen's playboys
on the bank of a big river,
she had washed up, by some favourable tide,
in the convent at Hosororo
on a shelf outside the chapel,
too scarred and far too crude
to go inside.

Madonna without child –
the oldest artifice of convenience;
so she could not keep her men
until the rumour of her golden breasts,
bruited on breezes across the sea,

became the text and ruse of recall
stirring in the hearts of wayward lovers,
those big in the books of history
or small like now and me.

Hungry at the heart of schoolrooms,
I throw my eyes back to that woman,
she who became this place
with he-goats grazing in her hair.
I looked and her smile was golden
like the last window of the west;
and the light of her smile
discoloured the big river;
and her red rush in the season of rains
discoloured the big river;
and the dust of the forest of her hair,
falling from the teeth of the sawmill,
discoloured the big river.
And I saw that her breasts,
her holy golden breasts,
were to be found underground,
beneath the skin of rivers,
within the bones of mountains.

Calling,
calling the adventurers home,
her voice sang in the river reeds,
in the sacred loaves of stone.
She, the dreamer of all dreams,
whose story is so often told,
conceives and bears another name:
Mac- or Immaculate
Mother of gold.

Come my lips and wide proclaim...

2

There is a flute, I dreamt,
within the horseman's thigh,
golden, slender as a reed, and he rode
like a strand of spider's web
blown against the sky. The ancient row
of sandstone hills curved like a hammock
in his eye. His dry lips curled
as he dreamt my dream
and he struck his silent thigh.

The son and horseman
dreamt he heard her call
and came with laughter in his limbs,
laughter loud like galloping hooves –
until an arrow came out of the sun,
traced rivers and hills on the map of his flesh
and he fell.

It was an old trick of earth
the trap of 'becoming mother':
the respectful bow turning into
the headlong fall, until,
prostrate on the measure of her memory,
the horseman sends his speech underground
in answer to drip and mutter –
so he becomes dumb.
And you will never look into eyes
that search only the ground
blinded of their laughter.
And you will never touch
those curled fingers groping for cavern,
for cracks in the stone of the sky,
forgetful of flute and gesture...
And this man with no utterance on earth
became the bridegroom of the golden woman –
the single object of oblivion,

sign-post or whipping-post of civilizations,
the native of desire.

And when you belong to his tribe
flutes will sprout from your curled fingers:
toys of the magician,
the entertainer of small boys
who can charm the rivers of space,
until flutes whisper in golden veins,
folding, moulding again
her sandstone into spirit.

On the banks of the big river the flutes danced,
commanding all the elements,
consuming the adventurers in fire.

And after the fire...

3

'No one appeared, it seemed,
on the shores of the lake.'
The language of history distorted the tale:
A lone fisherman came with a golden hook
and the fish he caught had a single scale
like primitive instruments
lost among stars. He read it correctly
in peace and in wars, but could utter
no word, so his silence endures.

The fisherman of words
waited in silence
on the shores of the lake,
his rod of golden dreams
erected high
above the mirror of the sky.
The slender string carried his silence,
the magic of his fingers, threading

the paradox of clouds beneath him,
harping in sunken cities
and the white bones of lost adventurers.

Images of depth awoke,
composed themselves into the creature,
and took the golden hook.
It may have felt the curve beneath its tongue,
the barb bitten deep;
but it tasted only
the tattered bait of longing
– like the stillness inside a storm –
and its eyes,
in the lethal air,
confessed all the stars,
all the lights of worlds,
and faded fast
like the memory of text or madonna wood,
like the sound of hooves
heard in the heart of schoolrooms,
signifying life and death.

Its single scale of being
was the numb, historic word:
the quantifying gauge of love and laughter.
The fisherman at sunset wheels
and sings to the universe
taking shape beneath his heel;
and his song is forever calling,
calling the secrets home.

And home is not the charisma of text,
but the shape of each word
that rolls from his tongue,
framing the songs of his mother and son
the galloping song and the song of the flute
and the songs that tell that his task is done,
or is nearly done,
or is never done...

And we call this home of his own desire
the secret language
of the golden man.

MASKS WITH VOICES

(for David Dabydeen)

Four Poems in the Manner of Mervyn Morris

I. SACRIFICE

Before I leap
(so willingly, my love)
upon that altar
where you stand, knife in hand,

permit me this prayer:
That you might hear
all the stories of my blood
before they stain the sand.

II. READING IN BED

Coming home late
and gently removing the book
open on your breast,
I searched for the sentence
where you fell asleep.

Waking up later
in the half-light
of the new day,
I read my own sentence
in the secret your body couldn't keep.

III.   RETALIATION

She was jealous of all the time
I was spending with Jean Rhys;
prying into letters,
savouring
the autobiographical flavour in
certain sentences,
musing about her sad eyes
and her hair
– all in the name of scholarship,
mind – but it irked her
to find 'that woman', though dead,
so constantly on my mind.

So I came home one day
to find myself
entirely out of favour
and her hopelessly,
hopelessly,
in love with Lope de Vega.

IV.   CAREFUL

'Be careful with that woman'
you said,
so I was careful.

But something went wrong. You see,
she was into being careless
with the likes of me.

An Old Woman Remembers

'He came from the west coast
I could picture him now,
him and his brother,
dressed in the fashion of that day:
Panama hats and canes
(Carrying cane and smelling like cane –
they father was a pan-boiler
on one of those west coast estates)
They would come to impress
and be impressed by town
two skinny boys, and so brown
from the week-long sun...
If they wuz wicked!
H'm. Interfering with all the girls...
But *him*, *he* had such charm –
and handsome!
Of course I was just a little thing then,
didn't take no notice of me –
then.
When we first married I used to
remind him of those days...
Oh go, child, don't make me talk
no more now, I old, but still got work
to do... He was a good man, God
rest his soul.'

Ol' Higue

You think I like this stupidness –
gallivanting all night without skin,
burning myself out like cane-fire
to frighten the foolish?
And for what? A few drops of baby blood?
You think I wouldn't rather
take my blood seasoned in fat
black-pudding, like everyone else?
And don't even talk 'bout the pain of salt
and having to bend these old bones down
to count a thousand grains of rice!

If only babies didn't smell so nice!
And If I could only stop
hearing the soft, soft call
of that pure blood running in new veins,
singing the sweet song of life
tempting an old, dry-up woman who been
holding her final note for years and years,
afraid of the dying hum...

Then again, if I didn't fly and come
to that fresh pulse in the middle of the night,
how would you, mother,
name your ancient dread?
And who to blame
for the murder inside your head..?
Believe me –
As long as it have women giving birth
a poor ol' higue like me can never dead.

Bone

The first fish in the first sea
with its big fin
broke the tight surface,
leaving its trailing wake
as the mould into which is poured
the pattern of all bone.
Hard, branched and sculptured white
into forms as brittle and eternal
as snow: rib-cage and herringbone
describe the wake
after the passage of flesh.
Eternal signatures of man and alley-cat,
intact through centuries of siege,
and washed up in wispy omens
against the closed blue lid
of the sky.

Horseman

Coming over the hill
with sheaves
of shoulder-slung moons
full like the riding pond
up, up and upon,
now over, now for ever
done.

Pale as mist, and limp
like morning's wavering reed,
he rode the strands of fading memory
where his mind and the moon recede.

Erect whatever monument...
Erect like the horseman's sword,
riding the pond over,
over the battle,
over now forever –
petrified in a city square
and (oh with what art!)
done.

Mantis Song

I'd like to think
that I will never be lost,
like all the others;
those that outlived your 'who'
and became your 'what' and 'where'.

I'd like to think
that even if I disappear
people would have the wit
to know I was there
from perturbations in your orbit
or the way you toss your hair.

    Consumed
    in your love,
    I'd like to think
    my love in you
    would bloom

Enigma
(for Victor Chang)

The language you speak
is not the language
your characters must speak,
and yet they seek
identity, comprehension.

Apprehension
concerning those who must read
a language they do not speak
leads you to seek
compromises.
And the surprise is
that every sentence you write
is a sentence passed
by unexpected judges,
initiates of a different rite.

To right
the historical wrongs
of all traffic in tongues
is beyond the power
of sentence, story,
novel-writing – and yet...
Olive reading *Summer Lightning!*
And yet...Bob Marley's songs!

Bonesong for a Silent Poet

You are the quiet man
who balances all my chatter
about bridges and things that matter
with your well of silence
that fixes me in its spell.

Sitting so still
in the shade of sea grape bushes
you look ever out
towards the reef's scrawled signature of foam
on the ruled horizon,
and, ruled again by your silent eye,
my thought's context of wave and sky
turns into the solid surf
of the interior of bone,
where all silence must have had its birth.

I once saw you stretch your hand
towards the disaster of a flute
hidden in a sunbather's thigh;
but you withdrew it, I breathed,
and you remained mute.

Words are not for everybody,
so I will sing your song:
make all the little noises of a life
while you gaze silently along
that line that tightens
over land and sea.

You be the silent centre
of my drum
– my horizon-keeper – and I
will hum for you, like waves,
a tune all your own...

until they learn to measure love,
until calipers close
around our song of bone.

Invitation to Tender

(Project Eldorado, Phase I:
clearing the site)

Place your ear to the thick wall of my chest,
gently – as on the rough bark of a tree;
listen to what my lips
can never tell: there is a deep down drum
that beats for you and me.

Place your thin lips, like a scar,
upon my cheeks – crisp as dried leaves
clinging to their stalks;
and ask then why I close my eyes and sigh:
you are the place where my fevered spirit walks.

Put your arm around the trunk of my neck,
and remind me that the flesh is warm
like the breathed vowels of your name;
then if you feel me sway beneath your touch
imagine I am bending in the storm.

Then swing your axe above my planted feet,
savour each stroke that severs earth from sky;
let the pain of love pierce your wooden hands.
And it is not for me that you must weep.
and it is not for you that I must die.

Penelope

As a young schoolboy
I always thought
of Penelope as a spider:
all that business of making
and unmaking the 'web'
which – I also thought –
was a sticky trap for the suitors.

Now I know differently:
Penelope threatens whenever I journey;
she becomes as real as any wife
left at home, working the loom
that woofs the filaments of my life
with her warped duties
– mother, stern preserver,
calm centre of all strife.

And now I know the web
is spun for me – a net
(baited with imaginary suitors)
to haul me home,
full of presents and regret
for having left Telemachus,
Penelope.... And yet,
sometimes I think it's all a trick
to wish me away again,
to emphasize my wrong
so that each minor dereliction
might live forever
in her immortal web of song.

Untilled

I bet you thought,
at first glance,
that this poem was 'untitled'
– that shop-worn, arty ploy
of minor poets. But no,
what I'm on about
is the word 'until',
used by my countrymen
as a farewell shout.
It rang in my ears
all those years ago
when I was pulling out:
'You catchin' tomorrow's plane,
well until...'
'Boy, I ent goin' see you again
before you go,
so until...'

A hundred times untilled,
I left to become as cultivated
as that homeland coast
that was fading far below
when I whispered the same valediction:
'Until...'
But the word creates a gap,
a huge silence,
and in that silence
me and my country are waiting
still.

Poem
(for Mervyn Morris)

Once, in a strange land,
Something glittered as I hurried by
And I stooped and poked about the sand,
Not thinking 'gold' or 'jewel'
But indulging an old susceptibility to light:

Something glittered
And I had to find the facet
that had fed my eye.

It turned out to be a stone
Ordinary, I thought at first, but worth keeping.
After an age in the soft oblivion of a pocket
It flashed like a sudden memory
Among keys and copper;
And each time since
I have seen a new dazzle
Until I cannot believe the polish,
The perfection of the thing.

It turned out to be a poem
And its light enriches me
(In all the strange lands where I live)
Far beyond the finite wealth of gold.

A POTARO QUARTET

(for Christopher Harrison)

Suspension Bridge

In the tight air
of early afternoon
the suspension bridge loomed:
twin curves of cable
described a monument of space,
the mind of a far, other place
(landscape isolated by a deed)
and that artificial tension
the engineers had decreed.

It was not clear
what was meant to be trapped
(or hallowed) by that net of air,
that harp of steel and wood
on whose frail, massive frame I stood:
I listened for vibrations in the air,
the river gave me back my puzzled glance;
neither knew what we had done
to deserve the temporary discord
of that moment's mute extravagance.

But moments pass
as the river passes ceaselessly
under the bridge, reflecting its harmonies
more faithfully than love.
And, as understanding comes
to all who stand above
such mirrored passion,
I became attuned to the meaning of that act:
suspension.

That sculpture strung
with my own nerves and nightmares
hummed with the suspensions of the age:
Suspension of the constitution,

Suspension of liberties,
of disbelief...
Suspended sentences, that left one free
to come to grief...

To fear the worst:
what if those cables burst!
It seemed the whole weight
of a country, past and future
(slave and free) stood balanced
above the river, on that bridge
between an afternoon's mirage
and all of history.

My own heart's oscillation
between panic and elation
matched the invisible amplitudes
of those towers:
I looked quickly at you,
a traveller coincident in time,
though distant
from the heart that felt these things.
You smiled – it was O.K. We took
two photographs and walked away.

After all the years I look again
upon these photos of two teenage boys
Dwarfed by that angelic instrument of a bridge
– the one a little pale from the hemorrhage
of certainty that befell him there,
and from a sense of fading privilege:
All travel beyond that moment
has been charged with the weight
of a country's misfortune;
all departures are uncertain,
each arrival seems too late.

Nightfall: Kangaruma

Arriving at Kangaruma
I was surprised by a new resthouse,
beds and an inexplicable sadness
in the afternoon light burning low
behind the trees. Off the river
came the coldest breeze that ever sliced
my fifteen years of life.

In a corner of the clear-
ing a red man with wild hair
squatted before a fire – porknocker,
someone surmised. I went over to inquire.
We talked as the sun died
about the river 'topside'; he showed me
a small cloudy diamond and
his manner warmed me,
reminded me of my father
– a foolish thought, for
he suddenly clutched my arm
with a hand as old and hard as diamond:
'life not easy on the water top.'
My nervous chuckle only fanned his fire:
'You think is fun?' he cried
'you think is fuckin' fun!'
His wild green eyes pierced
my foolish little life and I ran from him
with the last rays of the sun.

I sat alone on the verandah,
outside the circle of light
where the others talked loudly about women.
My porknocker's fire still burned
and once I saw his scarecrow shape
move across its light. I decided
I'd forgiven him, but I knew,

as the dark river wreathed us all,
that I had forgiven only myself;
and even that – in this hellish place –
was not beyond recall.

That night I dreamt about a man
– not my porknocker, this was black
as the river, yet an ordinary man;
shorter than I, perhaps
and certainly better dressed.
He had a sinister determination
to be good to me and pressed
a covered basket into my arms,
'Gifts,' he said: buxton spice,
avocado pear, cassava bread –
and a human heart.
When I recoiled he laughed:
'It's only a heart – just like yours'
And I remember being careful not to say
'I've never seen my heart,'
in case he felt he should oblige...

I woke in panic
to a darkness deeper than my dream;
covered in sweat I reached
into an adjoining bed and clutched
a sleeping arm: the first time
I'd let fear betray me...
'O God,' I breathed as I willed my heart to stop,
'Life is sheer terror on the water top.'

Plunge Pool: Amatuk

Dappled light
keeps track of waterfalls
like sprays of blossom
on the tree-trunk thrust of fingers
into the curtained cave beyond.

In torn envelopes of antique light
the coinage of the river rattles,
leaks and falls:
piece-bright silver and old gold
yellowing like a cat down rock stairs
where slivers of stoned glasshouses
(confirming my worst fears)
rush up in the rinse of clouds.

So the waterfall's whisper
(distinct from its roar)
was password to the dark cave of earth
where possibilities of birth
– gateway to the feather-strewn sky –
seemed brittle as the rasp of shells
on worn, stone basement forms
thrust up in shapely thigh.

White bones in watertight cupboards
grow in a spray of bubble light
to aerated furies of insight
that inflict blindness on my days
and wild obsessive dreams at night.

When I emerged
the applause of thunders
on the rainbow edge of sky
was for the sweep to diamond action
of my crane-winged, fish-finned, beloved diver,

gem-spangled doppelganger in full bloom
between the black tombs of rock and river.

Prismatic furnaces of light
each edge trailing cold fires
and the dust of blasted stars,
painted my porknocker's visions
in the fortuitous opacity of falls.

His hope in laden baskets
is hoisted beyond lips,
with the black river pursuing,
winnowing light through foam currents,
while preserving pockets of dusk
like remote perfumes –
as sprung flowers between river rocks
red rush in cycle with all dooms.

the river hones in its heart a mirror
where the acute body breaks in two/
into facets of my double desire:
His thorns of windblown hair
echoing the scourge of fire
seem remote and yet near,
as through the sights of rifles
aimed, like all earthly light,
at the sun.

And my son and porknocker
is split at thoughtless seams
pierced through the heart of light;
and the blood of love falls
in rain, in river, in waterfalls –
and when he re-enters the cave of earth
(poor brindled dog of light)
we often find,
when his dark fingers unfold like curled leaves:
the rough diamonds of love's plunge pool
and odd, tormented dreams.

Gorge

The kingfisher touches beaks
with its own reflection
in the river's bending mirror
near the lip of the waterfall.
The bubbled vein of secrets hurries over
the edge, to be lost – or encoded –
in that unforgettable thunder.
But nothing is that clear from under,
from the gorge that could so easily
become a labyrinth of self; I
(the pronoun instantly betrays me)
continued to reach for metaphor
where I've always felt at home;
but could not read the writing
on that white, tumbling wall
before my eyes. Sound, I decided,
must be all. So I heard again
the kingfisher, its whirr of wing
liberated by the black stones
that sliced the coded column, trans-
lating it back to river. But then
I could hear anything I listened for:
my father's voice, horses flashing past,
the whispering dead, Bach's B-minor mass...
That way lay madness, so I entered myself
as labyrinth, as deep gorge of words
waiting in ambush for the legions
of the future. I flung a shibboleth,
like a stone, to the foam-covered river,
stepped over the white bones of a shaman
disguised as the dead branches of a tree,
and entered that inner country:

Heartland of the gorge
where river horses flashed past,

their cataracting manes
and tails of foam combed
by black teeth of stone,
that flowed back in time
to where the falls first began
gnawing their way up-river –
like that insufferable old man
who has chewed his long beard
for centuries and spat
wisps of wet hair into my gorge...

Takes me back to the time
I stood on the second-floor landing
and tried to pee into a mayonnaise
bottle at the foot of the stairs:
'Are you mad?' were the only words
my father said to me when I
was hauled into his presence.
I didn't feel I could answer,
so he turned back to his papers;
but all my life I have heard that voice
questioning my sanity, and I wonder
if even death can reprieve me...

Dead people talk in whispers;
I meet them in dreams
and have to strain to hear
their tales of woe. They have all
been killed by their leaders:
scholars, priests, pot-bellied
wives and children – each has
a bullet to show, or a gash
in the side or yards of withered
or poisoned gut; but worst of all
is the whispering...

My country gorges itself on all like me,
as this river subsists on rock
and memory. Peace. A soft *Sanctus*

from lips of the living somehow
reaches me and hallows this place
where I cling to the wet
skirt of a waterfall:
(despite the poet) all
are not consumed. Not yet.